RiverStream Readers
Great Reading • Real Learning

Hard and Soft

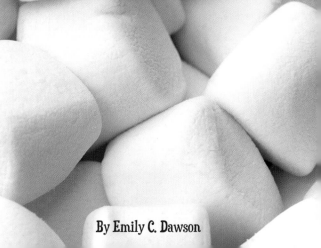

By Emily C. Dawson

RiverStream Readers
Great Reading • Real Learning

Learn to Read
Frequent repetition of sentence structures, high frequency words, and familiar topics provide ample support for brand new readers. Approximately 100 words.

Read Independently
Repetition is mixed with varied sentence structures and 6 to 8 content words per book are introduced with photo labels and picture glossary supports. Approximately 150 words.

Read to Know More
These books feature a higher text load with additional nonfiction features such as more photos, timelines, and text divided into sections. Approximately 250 words.

Accelerated Reader methodology uses Level A instead of Pre1. We have chosen to change it for ease of understanding by potential users.

Amicus Readers hardcover editions published by Amicus. P.O. Box 1329, Mankato, Minnesota 56002 www.amicuspublishing.us

U.S. publication copyright © 2012 Amicus. International copyright reserved in all countries. No part of this book may be reproduced in any form without written permission from the publisher.

Printed in the United States of America at Corporate Graphics, in North Mankato, Minnesota.

Series Editor   Rebecca Glaser
Series Designer   Christine Vanderbeek
Photo Researcher   Heather Dreisbach

RiverStream Publishing reprinted by arrangement with Appleseed Editions Ltd.

Library of Congress Cataloging-in-Publication Data
Dawson, Emily C.
Hard and soft / by Emily C. Dawson.
p. cm. – (Amicus readers. Let's compare)
Includes bibliographical references and index.
Summary: "A level A Amicus Reader that compares and contrasts common hard and soft objects, both in nature and man-made. Includes comprehension activity"–Provided by publisher.
ISBN 978-1-60753-000-8 (library bound)
1. Matter–Properties–Juvenile literature.
2. Touch–Juvenile literature. 3. Polarity–Juvenile literature. 4. Hardness–Juvenile literature. 5. English language–Synonyms and antonyms. I. Title.
QC173.16.D385 2011
530.4'12–dc22

2011005587

Photo Credits
Ho Yeow Hui/iStockphoto, cover top; Anthony Rosenberg/iStockphoto, cover botom; Mallory Samson /Gettylmages, 4; Peter38/Shutterstock, 6t; Lowe Llaguno/Shutterstock, 6b; Stephen Simpson/Gettylmages, 8t; Sneekerp I Dreamstime.com, 8b; Tony Tremblay/iStockphoto, 10t; arkanex/iStockphoto, 10b; greenland /Shutterstock, 12t; Fuse/Gettylmages, 12b; Ty Allison/Gettylmages, 14t; Cultura/Gettylmages, 14b; William Hart/Gettylmages, 16; Marilyn Nieves/iStockphoto, 18; AHMAD FAIZAL YAHYA/iStockphoto, 20m; Hughstoneian I Dreamstime.com, 20b; Elena Moiseeva I Dreamstime.com, 21t; Niels Quist Petersen/iStockphoto, 21b; VikaValter/iStockphoto, 22tl; Danny Smythe/iStockphoto, 22ml; Fenykepez/iStockphoto, 22bl; Алексей Брагин/iStockphoto, 22tr; Jaimie Duplass/Shutterstock, 22mr; David Morgan/iStockphoto, 22br

1 2 3 4 5 CG 15 14 13 12
RiverStream Publishing—Corporate Graphics, Mankato, MN—112012—1002CGF12

Table of Contents

Let's compare hard and soft.

Hard things are strong and firm. Soft things move and squish.

hard

Let's Compare!

soft

Cars drive on the hard road. Mr. Ryan's car gets stuck in the soft mud.

hard

Let's Compare!

soft

Macy walks on the hard rocks. Jon lies in the soft grass.

hard

Let's Compare!

soft

Kids skate on the hard ice. Paul rests in the soft snow.

hard

Let's Compare!

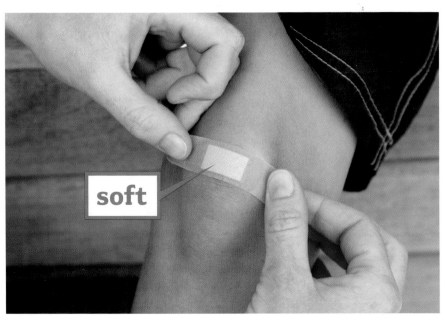

soft

Ethan fell on the hard sidewalk. A soft bandage helps his knee heal.

hard

Let's Compare!

soft

Alex runs on the hard track. Amy jumps on the soft mat.

hard

soft

Cole and Keisha's bunk beds are made of hard wood. Their blankets are made of soft cotton.

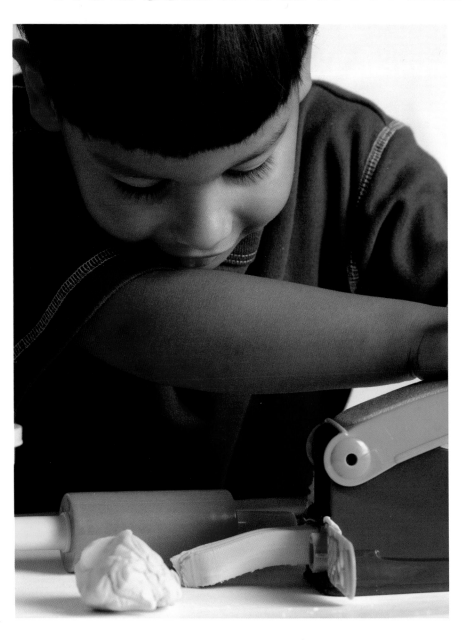

Hard things stay the same shape. Soft things bend. How do you use hard and soft things?

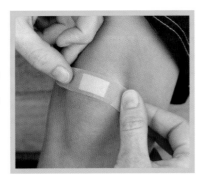

Picture Glossary

bandage →
a soft pad that covers
a scrape while it heals

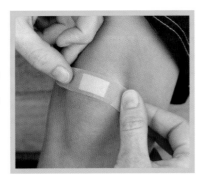

← **cotton**
soft cloth made from
the fluffy white fibers
of a plant

firm →
strong and not
able to bend

← squish
to change shape
when pressed

track →
a hard path for
running on

← wood
the hard material that
forms the trunk and
branches of a tree

Hard and Soft

Look at the photos.
1. Which things are hard?
2. Which things are soft?
3. Which things do you use together?

Ideas for Parents and Teachers

Books 1 through 5 in the RiverStream Readers Level Pre 1 Series give children the opportunity to compare familiar concepts with lots of reading support. Repetitive sentence structures, familiar vocabulary, and photo labels reinforce concepts in the text. In each book, the picture glossary defines new vocabulary and the "Let's Compare" activity page reinforces compare and contrast techniques.

Before Reading
- Ask the child about the difference between hard and soft. Ask: What things are hard? What things are soft? How do you know?
- Discuss the cover photo. What do these photos tell them?
- Look at the picture glossary together. Read and discuss the words. Ask the child to sort the photos into a hard group and a soft group.

Read the Book
- "Walk" through the book and look at the photos. Ask questions or let the child ask questions about the photos.
- Read the book to the child or have him or her read independently.
- Show him or her how to read the photo labels and refer back to the picture glossary to understand the full meaning.

After Reading
- Have the child identify hard and soft things around the room.
- Prompt the child to think more, asking questions such as Why are some things hard and some things soft? Why is a library book hard? Why is a couch soft? Why are they made that way?

Index

Web Site

Compare and Contrast Theme Page
http://www.enchantedlearning.com/themes/compare.shtml

SHERLOCK HOLMES
vs.
DRACULA

JOHN H. WATSON, M.D., M.B., B.S., M.R.C.S., was born in England in 1852, and was friend, confidant, and chronicler of the great detective, Mr Sherlock Holmes, whose exploits have served to inspire generations of amateur sleuths around the world since their first publication in the *Strand* magazine in the late 1890s. In 1878 he took his medical degree at the University of London and shortly after served as assistant surgeon with the Fifth Northumberland Fusiliers in Afghanistan. There he transferred to the Berkshires, and was severely wounded in the Battle of Maiwand, after which he left the service and returned to London. While there, he began his long association with Sherlock Holmes, who became the subject of his more than sixty published books and articles. Dr Watson died in 1940.

LOREN D. ESTLEMAN is a graduate of Eastern Michigan University and a veteran police-court journalist. Since the publication of his first novel in 1976, he has established himself as a leading writer of both mystery and western fiction. His western novels include Golden Spur Award winner *Aces and Eights*, *Mister St. John*, *The Stranglers*, and *Gun Man*. His Amos Walker, Private Eye series includes *Motor City Blue*, *Angel Eyes*, *The Midnight Man*, *The Glass Highway*, Shamus Award winner *Sugartown*, *Every Brilliant Eye*, *Lady Yesterday*, *Downriver*, and *The Hours of the Virgin*; the most recent Walker mystery, *A Smile on the Face of the Tiger*, was published in August 2000. Estleman lives in Michigan with his wife, Deborah, who writes under the name Deborah Morgan.

AVAILABLE NOW

ALFRED HITCHCOCK MYSTERIES
The Vertigo Murders

AMOS WALKER MYSTERIES
by Loren D. Estleman
Motor City Blue
Angel Eyes
The Midnight Man

MASAO MASUTO MYSTERIES
Masuto Investigates: Volume 1
by Howard Fast

MOSES WINE MYSTERIES
by Roger L. Simon
The Big Fix
Wild Turkey
The Lost Coast

OTTO PENZLER HOLLYWOOD MYSTERIES
Laura
by Vera Caspery

PHILIP MARLOWE MYSTERIES
Raymond Chandler's Philip Marlowe
Anthology; Byron Preiss, Editor

SHERLOCK HOLMES MYSTERIES
Revenge of the Hound
by Michael Hardwick

TOBY PETERS MYSTERIES
by Stuart M. Kaminsky
Murder on the Yellow Brick Road
The Devil Met a Lady
Never Cross a Vampire

COMING SOON

She Done Him Wrong
A Toby Peters Mystery
by Stuart M. Kaminsky

Peking Duck
A Moses Wine Mystery
by Roger L.Simon

The Glass Highway
An Amos Walker Mystery
by Loren D. Estleman